C is for Cornhusker

A Nebraska Alphabet

Written by Rajean Luebs Shepherd and Illustrated by Sandy Appleoff

Sleeping Bear Press
310 North Main Street, Suite 300
Chelsea, MI 48118
www.sleepingbearpress.com

© 2004 Thomson Gale, a part of the Thomson Corporation.

Thomson, Star Logo and Sleeping Bear Press are trademarks
and Gale is a registered trademark used herein under license.

Printed and bound in Canada.

10 9 8 7 6 5 4 3 2 1

Library of Congress Cataloging-in-Publication Data

Shepherd, Rajean Luebs.
C is for cornhusker : a Nebraska alphabet / written by Rajean Luebs Shepherd ;
illustrated by Sandy Appleoff.
p. cm.
ISBN 1-58536-147-X
1. English language—Alphabet—Juvenile literature. 2. Nebraska—Juvenile
literature. I. Appleoff, Sandy. II. Title.
F666.3.S54 2004
978.2—dc22   2004005258

In loving memory of Grandpa Henry Luebs,
who was born in 1895 on a homestead in Wood River, Nebraska.

A heartfelt thank you to:
my husband Stuart and sons Breton and Collin...the loves of my life.
my wonderful parents...for teaching me, "If at first you don't succeed, try, try again!"
Up with People...for the memories of a lifetime.
Sleeping Bear Press, Amy Lennex,
and Sandy Appleoff...for making a dream come true!

RAJEAN

Haizly and Dottie B, with special thanks to Helen Ravenhill,
Justin Newhouse, and the entire Appleoff family.

SANDY

≈

"So every man, woman and child shall be able to say, on coming
as I have come, towards the evening of life, in all sincerity
and truth, if you seek my monument, look around you!"

J. STERLING MORTON
ARBOR DAY 1894

In pioneer days, the Nebraska Territory was almost treeless. However, Julius Sterling Morton, a journalist and politician from Nebraska City, changed that when he proposed setting aside a special day, each year, for planting trees. Mr. Morton said, "Trees provide food for the table, wood for the stove, shade for the body, and beauty for the soul." On April 10, 1872, the first Arbor Day was celebrated and Nebraskans planted over one million trees, including cottonwood, Nebraska's official state tree. Today, all 50 states celebrate Arbor Day, as do other countries.

In 1902, the year that J.S. Morton died, President Theodore Roosevelt established Nebraska National Forest, the largest hand-planted forest in the United States.

Today many visitors tour the Morton's 52-room mansion at beautiful Arbor Lodge State Historical Park, especially on Arbor Day.

Let's travel the state of Nebraska
and begin with the letter A.
For the planting of trees to help Mother Earth,
it's known as Arbor Day.

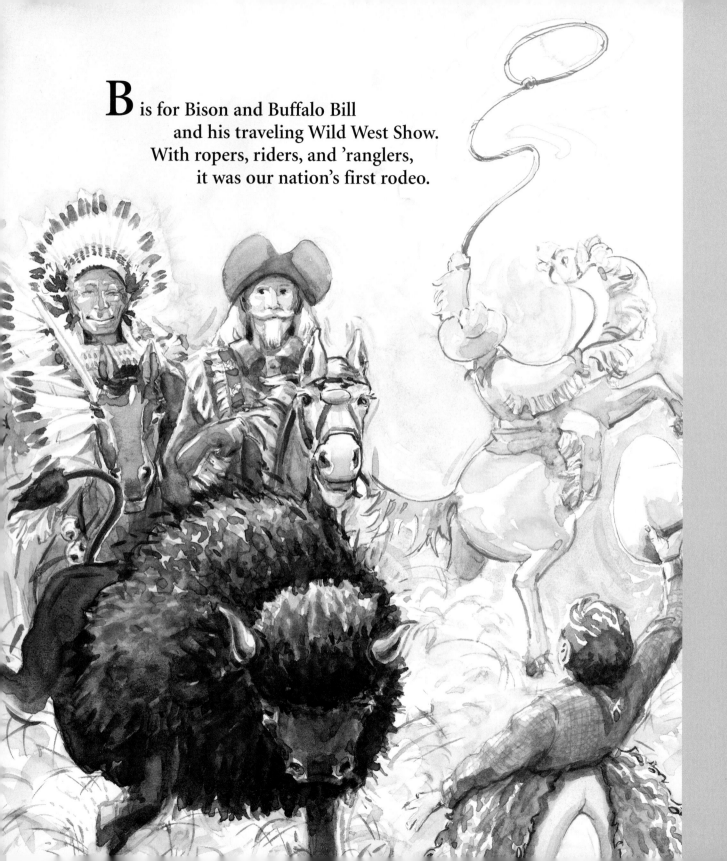

B is for Bison and Buffalo Bill
  and his traveling Wild West Show.
With ropers, riders, and 'ranglers,
  it was our nation's first rodeo.

Born in Iowa in 1846, William Frederick
Cody is a legend in the history of the
American West. He was an expert rider
and rifleman and his skill as a buffalo
hunter earned him his nickname, "Buffalo
Bill." He once claimed to have shot 4,280
buffalo while working as a buffalo hunter
for the men building the first railroad.

In 1882 William Cody staged America's
first rodeo, Old Glory Blowout, at his
Scout's Rest Ranch in North Platte,
Nebraska, now a state historical park. He
then took his wild and woolly frontier
show throughout the United States
and Europe.

Cody died in 1917, but his legend lives on
in many books, TV westerns, and in North
Platte's annual events of "Christmas at
the Cody's," held at his Victorian mansion
and the "Buffalo Bill Rodeo" held during
NEBRASKAland Days.

Cornhusker begins with the letter C.
It's the nickname of our state.
And for the crops and cattle,
that make this land so great.

In 1895 Nebraska was nicknamed the Tree Planter's State in honor of Arbor Day, but in 1945 the legislature changed it to the "Cornhusker State" because of the importance of corn. The name, coined in 1900, is derived from the nickname for the University of Nebraska athletic teams, the "Cornhuskers." A cornhusker is someone who peels the husks of corn by hand, which was a common method of harvesting before modern machinery.

Nebraska is known as a leading farming and ranching state where a larger percentage of total land is used for producing crops and livestock than in any other state. As Willa Cather, the Pulitzer Prize-winning author from Red Cloud, Nebraska, expressed it, "Elsewhere the sky is the roof of the world, but here the earth is the floor of the sky."

Dd

Each spring the skies of Nebraska dance alive with the amazing sights and sounds of the world's largest gathering of sandhill cranes. Eighty percent of the world's population, approximately 500,000 birds, make the migratory journey from Mexico and the southern United States to the northern parts of Canada, Alaska, and Siberia.

Nebraska takes its name from its outstanding natural feature, the Platte River. Native Americans called the shallow, braided river "nebrathka," meaning flat or broad water. This official state river is a favorite rest stop for the migrating sandhill cranes, where they parachute to the ground with their dangling legs. Here they feed on delicacies while roosting on the river sandbars, where they are protected from their predators. They also feast on a banquet of grain from the nearby cornfields.

The spirit of these stately, long-legged, long-necked birds is best characterized by the amusement of their captivating dance that includes bowing, arching, leaping, and stick tossing.

D is the Dance of sandhill cranes,
as they bow and leap and fling.
Half a million come to roost,
when they migrate north each spring.

In 1803 President Thomas Jefferson bought a large expanse of land, west of the Mississippi River, from France. This sale, known as the Louisiana Purchase, doubled the size of the new nation. President Jefferson then chose army officers Meriwether Lewis and William Clark to explore the new territory and search for an east-west water route connecting the Atlantic Ocean to the Pacific Ocean.

The expedition, known as the Corps of Discovery began in May 1804 on the Missouri River, in a keelboat and two pirogues or dugout canoes, and followed what is now the eastern border of Nebraska. En route, Lewis and Clark met Sacagawea, a Shoshone Indian, who became an important interpreter and guide.

Lewis and Clark did not discover the fabled Northwest Passage on their 8,000-mile roundtrip journey, which lasted over two years. However, through detailed observations, recorded in their journals, they succeeded in sharing their knowledge of Native American tribes, geography, plants and animals, and paved the way for future explorers.

E is the early Explorers
who up the Missouri embarked
on an exciting expedition
led by Lewis and Clark.

F is for Febold Feboldson,
    the tall tale of our state.
He made a "beeline" for the border
    and that's why it is so straight.

Nebraska's own folk hero, Febold Feboldson, set out to accomplish the ta[sk] of making a perfect southern border [for] Nebraska after Paul Bunyan had faile[d]. The "tall tale" claims that Paul Bunyan a[nd] his blue ox, Babe, plowed a furrow bu[t it] was so crooked that it filled with water [to] become the Republican River. So Feb[old] Feboldson then spent 15 years crossi[ng] eagles with honeybees, Nebraska's sta[te] insect. This finally produced the large[st] strongest insects known as "beeagles[,"] and he harnessed them to his plow, making a "beeline" for the border. Thus[,] he succeeded in making a straight bord[er] between Nebraska and Kansas and proved that nothing is impossible!

Great Plains begins with the letter **G**,
where homesteaders toiled the land
of one hundred sixty acres
that were cultivated by hand.

Four-fifths of Nebraska is part of the U.S. geographic region known as the Great Plains. To encourage settlement on this vast and empty frontier, often referred to as the Great American Desert, President Lincoln signed the Homestead Act of 1862. "Free Land!" was the cry that allowed any man or woman to lay claim to 160 acres of prairie by settling and cultivating it. After five years, settlers "proved up" by showing they had met the requirements, including U.S. citizenship, and the land was theirs. With the Homestead Act, the Great Plains became a new land of opportunity for thousands of Americans and European immigrants.

Daniel Freeman, a Civil War soldier, is recognized as the first person to apply for a land grant shortly after the Homestead Act went into effect. Today, visitors can tour Homestead National Monument, the site of Daniel Freeman's claim, near Beatrice, Nebraska.

G g

H is for Horses on the Pony Express
and the men who braved the ride.
They delivered mail in record time
across the countryside.

Begun on April 3, 1860, the Pony Express stretched 2,000 miles from St. Joseph, Missouri to San Francisco, California and mail was successfully delivered in 10 days. Relay stations were set up about every 10 to 15 miles across the route. Riders changed horses at these stations and then continued on their nearly 100-mile section before handing their leather mochila, or mail bag, on to the next rider. The Pony Express charged five dollars per half-ounce for mail (about $85 in today's money), later reducing the fee to one dollar.

Although the Pony Express lasted only 18 months, when it was replaced by the telegraph, it was an important part of Nebraska's history in linking the East with the West.

Many Pony Express stations still exist in Nebraska today, including the Rock Creek Station, which is part of the Pony Express National Historic Trail.

The mammoth is Nebraska's state fossil and one of the largest mammoths ever discovered was found in Nebraska. "Archie" is on display at the State Museum in Lincoln and stands over 15 ½ feet tall!

During the Ice Age, great herds of mammoths, rhinoceros, camels, and bison roamed the area. Today Nebraska is one of the greatest time capsules for fossils and there are many archaeological sites where visitors can get a three-dimensional look into ancient times.

Agate Fossil Beds National Monument, a large fossilized waterhole, has hundreds of preserved skeletons, including a ferocious "Terrible Pig" 10 feet long.

Prehistoric mammals, mainly rhinoceros, died 12 million years ago from a blanket of volcanic ash. They can be seen up close still locked in their death poses at Ashfall Fossil Beds State Historical Park.

The Hudson-Meng Bison Bonebed excavation provides clues to the mystery of 600 bison that perished 10,000 years ago.

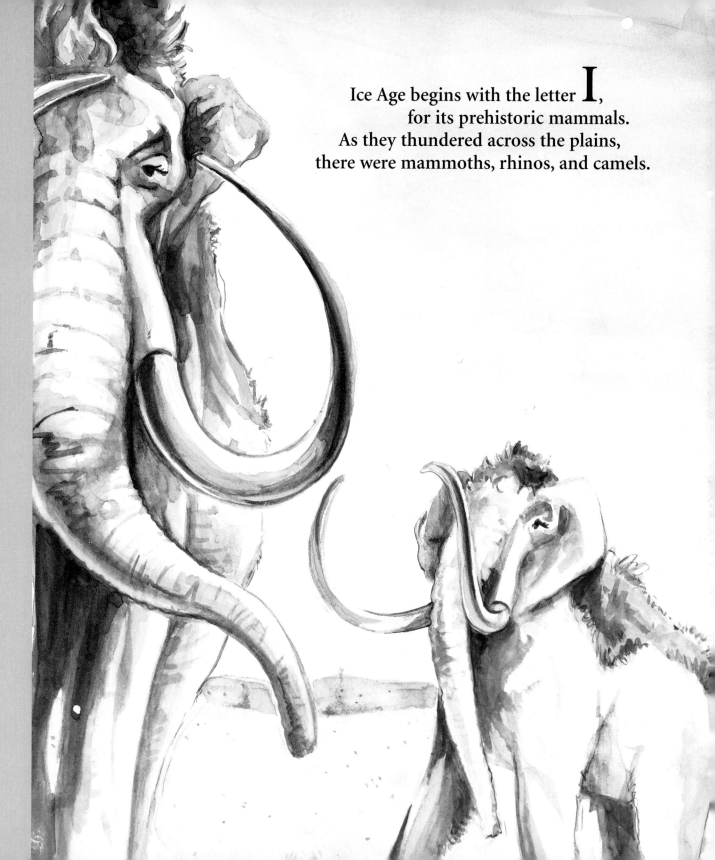

Ice Age begins with the letter I,
for its prehistoric mammals.
As they thundered across the plains,
there were mammoths, rhinos, and camels.

During the mid-1800s nearly 500,000 pioneers went "westering" with handcarts and covered wagons, or prairie schooners, for different reasons. Some were seeking gold, others were fleeing religious persecution, but most were searching for new land to farm. Regardless of their starting point or their final destination, they all converged in the Platte River Valley of Nebraska on their way west to California, Utah, or Oregon.

Along the trails, Nebraska's towering geologic formations of Chimney Rock, Scotts Bluff, Courthouse Rock, and Jail Rock became four of the most spectacular and celebrated landmarks to be recorded in the pioneers' journals.

Without the pioneers' journey and their spirit of daring and determination, America would not be the country it is today.

Now J is the pioneers' Journey.
In wagons they traveled west.
On the Mormon and Oregon Trails,
they began an adventurous quest.

J j

5¢ a glass

There's a delicious drink that begins with **K**
and Kool-Aid® is its name.
With so many colors and flavors,
it's one of Nebraska's claims.

Edwin Perkins was a young inventor and entrepreneur who loved creating concoctions in his mother's kitchen. In 1927, while living in Hastings, he developed a method for making Kool-Aid®. The powder originally sold for 10 cents a packet and came in a rainbow of six original flavors: cherry, grape, lemon-lime, orange, raspberry, and strawberry. During the Great Depression Mr. Perkins sold the packets for five cents and Kool-Aid® stands began to pop up across the country. By 1950, nearly one million packets were produced each day.

Today the original Kool-Aid® man costume, worn in TV commercials, is part of the Kool-Aid®: *Discover the Dream* exhibit at the Hastings Museum and the world's largest Kool-Aid® stand, 75 feet long, is on display during Kool-Aid® Days in Hastings. Nebraska's official soft drink is Kool-Aid®, and it continues to bring smiles to thirsty drinkers around the world.

Let's visit the capital city
which begins with the letter **L**.
Named for our 16th president,
it's Lincoln, could you tell?

In 1867, soon after becoming the 37th
state in the Union, the capital of Nebraska
was renamed Lincoln to honor the recently
assassinated President Abraham Lincoln.
When completed in 1932, the majestic
capitol building, described as the Tower
of the Plains, was the first in the nation
designed as an art deco skyscraper and it
has been called a "modern architectural
wonder." The gold-glazed 400-foot tower
is topped by a 19-foot statue of The Sower
scattering the seeds of agriculture, life,
hope, and prosperity.

Nebraska's unicameral form of govern-
ment is unique in the United States. The
other 49 state legislatures are divided
into two houses, the senate and house
of representatives, but Nebraska has
only one house, the senate. The state
motto is "Equality before the law."

M is a Museum and Monument
that spans across the road,
welcoming visitors to our state
with its history to be told.

The Great Platte River Road Archway Monument, near Kearney, is a gateway to the West that soars 11 stories above Interstate 80. Built to resemble the frontier forts of the region, which now serve as state historical parks and museums, the "archway to the past" houses interactive exhibits of the many trails of history and heritage that converged in the Platte River Valley.

Today visitors can step back in time at many other fascinating Nebraska museums. Attend school in a one-room schoolhouse at Stuhr Museum, one of America's largest living-history attractions. Ride the country's oldest steam-powered merry-go-round at Pioneer Village with its 50,000 items showing human progress since 1830. Walk aboard a 55-foot keel-boat replica at the Missouri River Basin Lewis and Clark Interpretive Center. Sleep in a Native American earth lodge and see prehistoric fossils and artifacts at Dancing Leaf Earth Lodge. Treasures await in Nebraska's museums!

m
M

The Niobrara, a national scenic river, travels through the quiet and unspoiled beauty of northern Nebraska. The river winds a course through the vast Sandhills region of grass-covered sand dunes, the largest in North America. It also meanders through wilderness refuges and preserves designated to protect the wildlife of six distinct ecosystems. This area is also home of the Cowboy Trail, one of the longest rail-to-trail projects in the United States with its 320 miles of hiking, biking, and horseback riding trails.

In summer the Niobrara leisurely flows, carrying giant innertubes, canoes, and kayaks past the ever-changing scenery of ranches, forests, sandstone canyons, and waterfalls. This region is Nebraska's "waterfall capital" and Smith's Falls is the state's tallest at 70 feet.

Another popular summer spot, Lake McConaughy, features more than 100 miles of beautiful, white sandy beaches. Nicknamed "Big Mac," the lake is located near the "Cowboy Capital" of Ogallala.

N
n

N is the Niobrara,
      a popular summer spot,
  for floating down the river
 when the weather gets too hot!

O

O is the city of Omaha,
　　　　with its Boys Town home and school.
Founded by Father Flanagan,
　　　　there, love is the Golden Rule.

Omaha, Nebraska's largest city, has a rich cultural environment with many attractions including the Joslyn Art Museum, Strategic Air and Space Museum, NCAA College World Series of baseball, and the world-renowned Boys Town.

Edward Flanagan was born in Ireland, but in 1917 he began a career that made him "an international symbol of spiritual and material hope for millions." With $90 borrowed from a friend, Father Flanagan rented a house to care for homeless and underprivileged boys. His belief was that all children could be successful if they are praised, admired, and trained by example to do what is right.

In 1938 actor Spencer Tracy won an Academy Award for his portrayal of Father Flanagan in the film, *Boys Town*. The Oscar is on display at Boys Town.

Although Father Flanagan died in 1948, Boys Town has grown to a more than 1,000-acre campus for both boys and girls and proved the power of love can change everything.

Powwow begins with the letter P.
It's a cultural celebration,
   with colorful regalia and tribal dancing,
of the Native American Nations.

Nebraska is rich with Native American culture and history and it is the site of the Omaha, Ponca, Santee Sioux, and Winnebago tribes. Crazy Horse and Red Cloud were two famous leaders of the Oglala Sioux tribe. Dr. Susan LaFlesche Picotte, of the Omaha tribe, was the country's first Native American woman to become a medical doctor.

Throughout the summer months, the Nebraska tribes celebrate Native American rituals and traditions with dancing, singing, drumming, and colorful regalia of the powwow. Each dance performed at a powwow has its own style but one of the oldest expressions of a traditional culture is the Grass Dance. The regalia of the dancer is decorated with long, colorful fringe which depicts the tall, blowing grass on the prairie. This enhances the graceful moves of the dancers' bodies as they sway in the imaginary breeze. No other event captures the Native American spirit like the social celebration of the powwow.

Q

Q is a Quilt of many designs,
a history woven in thread.
Weaving its tale of long ago,
as it lays upon the bed.

The patchwork designs of many quilts
have a story to tell of the days of long
ago. Pioneer life was not easy and as
settlers packed up their belongings to
move west toward Nebraska, they took
many quilts with them for different
purposes. Quilts were often used to keep
the family valuables from breaking on
the bumpy wagon ride and they also
served as cushions and beds. Once the
pioneers were settled on the prairie,
quilts added color to the home and
served as protection from the cold and
stormy winters. Pioneer families were
proud of their quilts and many were
created and named for special events
in their lives.

One of the world's largest quilt collections
is on display at the International Quilt
Study Center in Lincoln. These quilts have
helped preserve the story of our nation
in a very special art form.

If you visit the University of Nebraska in Lincoln on a Saturday in fall, there is nothing quite like the spectacle of a Huskers' football game. More than 76,000 cheering fans, dressed in a sea of red and white, or the official colors scarlet and cream, fill Memorial Stadium to make it the third largest "city" in the state. There have been consecutive sellout games since November 1962.

Nebraskans are famed for their loyalty to the five-time national football champion team whose motto is:

"not the victory, but the action;
not the goal, but the game;
in the deed, the glory."

Lincoln is also home of the first patented roller skate from 1819. It can be found among the world's largest collection of historical roller skates at the National Museum of Roller Skating.

R is the Red of the Huskers' team
and the football fans who cheer.
"Go Big Red!" in the stadium,
is an amazing sound to hear.

Rr

The first task of the pioneers who settled on the vast frontier was finding shelter. Since trees were scarce, settlers were forced to use the prairie itself for building material. Oxen and horse-drawn plows were used to cut the thick ribbons of grass and soil called sod or "Nebraska marble." The sod was then cut into giant bricks to build "soddies" or sod houses. A soddy was inexpensive to build and it was solid and safe from prairie grass fires. The thick walls kept the dwelling warm in winter and cool in summer.

Living in a sod house had its disadvantages, too. During rainstorms, the leaky roof required mothers to hold umbrellas over the stove while cooking. Children gathered buffalo or cow chips, dried pats of manure, to be used for fuel in the stove. Uninvited guests such as bugs, mice, snakes, and even grazing cows unexpectedly dropped in from the grass-covered roof overhead.

Sod house begins with the letter S,
a first home for the pioneers.
With walls of dirt and a roof of grass,
it weathered many years.

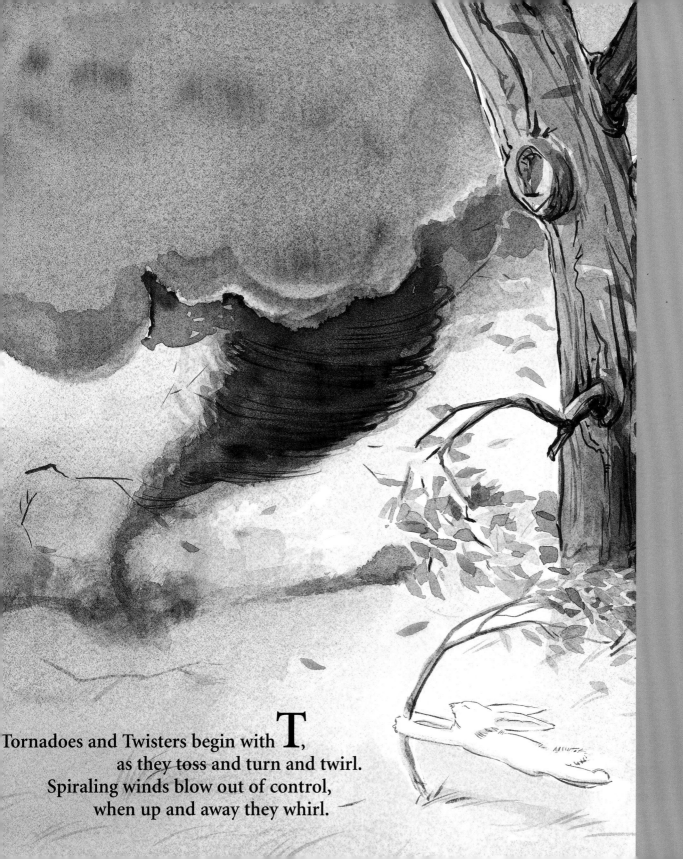

Tornadoes and Twisters begin with T,
        as they toss and turn and twirl.
Spiraling winds blow out of control,
        when up and away they whirl.

No part of the United States has had more varied or unpredictable weather than the Great Plains, including floods, drought, dust storms, prairie fires, blizzards, hailstorms, tornadoes, and even grasshopper invasions. Nebraskans are often heard saying, "If you don't like the weather, just wait a minute!"

In late spring, warm moist air begins to move up from the Gulf of Mexico and meets cool upper air from Canada, causing tornadoes to churn in "Tornado Alley." Tornadoes often bring hail and Nebraska has recorded some of the largest on record—hailstones the size of cantaloupes.

During June 1980, the area of Grand Island was hit by seven tornadoes in one evening, a storm unlike any seen before on the Great Plains. This event became a well-known book and TV movie, *Night of the Twisters.*

Now it's clickety clack down the railroad track
and on to the letter U,
for the trains of the Union Pacific
with their cars and freight and crew.

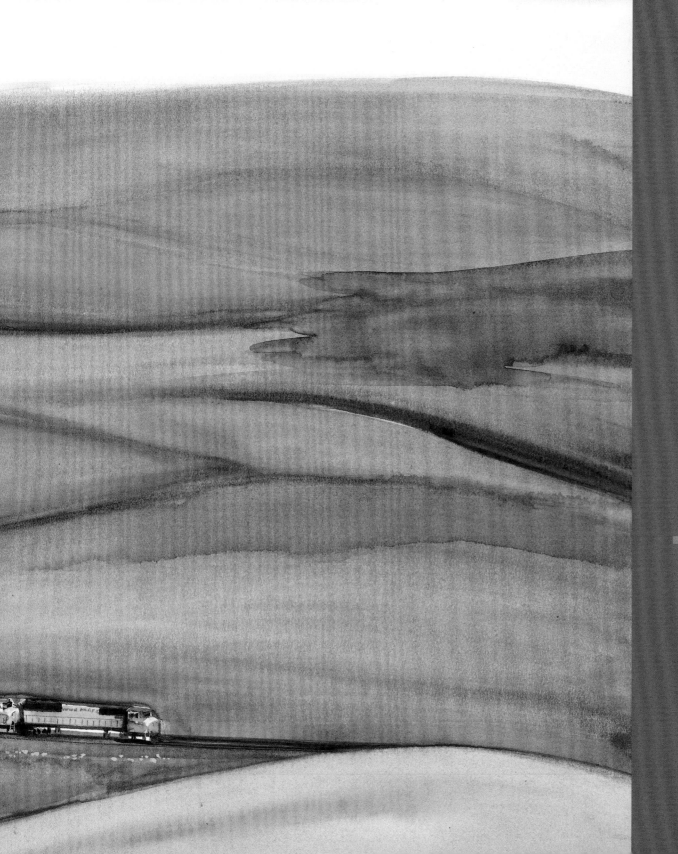

A major factor in the settlement of Nebraska was the building of the "Iron Road," the first transcontinental railroad, from Omaha, Nebraska to Sacramento, California. By promising free land and successful farming, Union Pacific recruited emigrants from the East and immigrants from Europe to settle along railroad routes in the Nebraska Territory.

Union Pacific's Bailey Yard in North Platte is the largest classification railroad yard in the world and was officially recognized in the *Guinness Book of World Records* in 1995. Every 24 hours, 10,000 railroad cars are sorted and sent toward their final destinations. If the University of Nebraska Huskers were to play at Bailey Yard, they would have room for 3,097 football fields!

The national headquarters of the Union Pacific Railroad is located in Omaha, with the Union Pacific Railroad Museum in nearby Council Bluffs, Iowa.

Uu

V is for the canteen Volunteers
who served during World War II,
as six million soldiers were greeted and fed
when their trains came passing through.

From December 1941 until April 1946, miraculous events took place in a small town in Nebraska. With the help of 125 nearby communities, the North Platte Canteen operated for 51 consecutive months to provide food, warmth, and friendship to six million soldiers on their way to war.

During the brief 10 to 15 minute stop, soldiers were greeted and fed by volunteers who provided coffee, sandwiches, fried chicken, hard-boiled eggs, birthday cakes, care packages, and a spirit of love in an unexpected place far from home. With an average of 23 trains and 3,000 to 5,000 troops per day, this was an amazing feat during wartime rationing.

The canteen was often filled with music, dancing, and merriment before the train whistle signaled departure and a final cheery message like, "God bless and keep you, goodbye, and hurry back," could be heard.

With few trees and hills on the Nebraskan plains, a constant wind was an ever-present feature of prairie weather. By harnessing the free and limitless power of the wind, a windmill was able to perform many valuable services. For the settlers, the windmill provided running water for drinking and bathing and served as a weather indicator and a lookout tower. On the land, it greened the pasture, grew the fruit trees and crops, and watered the cattle. This multipurpose machine enabled farmers and ranchers to thrive where life would otherwise have been impossible.

Today Nebraska's windmills are still used to pump water from the Ogallala Aquifer, the nation's largest underground water supply. The aquifer is key to the bountiful agriculture of Nebraska and if pumped over the United States, the aquifer could cover all 50 states with 1 ½ feet of water.

Let's visit the letter **W**,
for "skyscrapers of the prairie."
They're known as giant Windmills,
though their size and shape may vary.

The Underground Railroad was a secret network of trails and places, including Mayhew Cabin in Nebraska City, where Freedom Seekers could receive assistance in their journey north to freedom.

The Mayhew Cabin, built in 1852, is one of the state's oldest standing treasures, a cottonwood log cabin with a wonderful history. Due to John Brown's abolitionist activity here and the cabin's strategic position next to the Missouri River and the free state of Iowa's border, the cabin became an important site on the Underground Railroad.

Stories have been told of Freedom Seekers hiding in the Mayhew's cellar, locally known as John Brown's Cave. This cellar was located in the bank of a nearby creek where produce from the Mayhew's vineyard was kept. Mrs. Mayhew frequently served breakfast of cornbread to the Freedom Seekers before they took the first dawn ferryboat across the Missouri River into the free state of Iowa and ultimately to real freedom in Canada.

X marks the spot of a hiding place
sometimes known as John Brown's Cave,
on the Underground Railroad, an important site,
for freedom-seeking slaves.

Y is the Yellow of our meadowlark
    and our cottonwood trees in fall,
        the goldenrods and the honeybees,
        state symbols one and all.

Yy

The western meadowlark, Nebraska's state bird, is the farmer's friend because it often feeds on the grasshoppers that destroy the crops. It is known for its joyful song.

On the treeless prairie, cottonwood shoots were often collected by the settlers who planted them on their homestead claims. In autumn, the shaking, shimmering leaves of the cottonwood, Nebraska's state tree, turn brilliant yellow.

Nebraska's state flower, the goldenrod, is a wildflower that grows almost everywhere in the state. The bright yellow flower grows in clusters at the top of the stem and represents the hardy endurance of Nebraska's pioneers.

The honeybee became Nebraska's state insect after a suggestion by schoolchildren in Auburn, Nebraska. Beekeeping came to the state during the covered wagon era and it has become one of the state's great industries.

Other official state symbols include the cotton-tailed deer, the state mammal, and the channel catfish, the state fish.

Take a walk on the wild side at the zoo in Omaha with its thousands of unique and exotic animals. Sharks and other sea creatures can be viewed up close and personal in the walk-through tunnel of the Scott Aquarium. Fascinating animals can be seen in the Desert Dome, the world's largest indoor desert, and in the Lied Jungle, the world's largest indoor tropical rain forest. Night creatures come to life and mysteries of the darkness are revealed in the world's largest nocturnal exhibit, "Kingdoms of the Night." The main objectives of this world-class zoo are conservation, research, education, and recreation.

Other zoos in the state include Wildlife Safari, Folsom Children's Zoo, Riverside Zoo, and Northeast Nebraska Zoo. As you can see, a wildlife adventure awaits you in the great state of Nebraska!

Our journey ends with the letter Z
for the Henry Doorly Zoo,
Where rain forest, desert, and night creatures
are waiting just for you!

As I've traveled the state of Nebraska
and journeyed from A to Z,
I've discovered so many treasures,
so much to do and see.
But of all the wonderful sights
and the history that abounds,
the spirit of Nebraskans
is the greatest treasure I've found.

A Friendly Farmer's Field of Facts

1. What is the name of the special day set aside for the caring and planting of trees, first celebrated in Nebraska on April 10, 1872?

2. William Frederick Cody, who was nicknamed "Buffalo Bill," started our nation's first _____ in Nebraska.

3. What is Nebraska's state nickname and why?

4. Over 500,000 of these long-legged, long-necked birds land in Nebraska, each spring, on their migration north. Can you name this bird?

5. The explorers, Lewis and Clark, began their expedition in 1804 on the _____ River, which forms the eastern border of Nebraska.

6. According to the "tall tale," who made the southern border of Nebraska straight by harnessing "beeagles" to a plow and making a "beeline" for the border?

7. To encourage settlement on the vast plains of the Nebraska Territory, how many acres of land were settlers given under the Homestead Act of 1862?

8. The dinosaur is Nebraska's official state fossil. True or False?

9. The capital city of Nebraska was named for which president?

10. Nebraska, the 37th state, is the only "unicameral" state in the country. What is the meaning of the word?

11. What is the name of the official soft drink of Nebraska, developed by Edwin Perkins?

12. Describe a Native American powwow.

13. How many people fill the football stadium at the University of Nebraska, on game day, to make it the third largest city in the state?

14. Who founded the world-renowned home and school for children in Omaha, originally known as Boys Town?

15. Name one of Nebraska's geologic landmarks that helped guide the pioneers along the Oregon and Mormon Trails.

16. Why did the first settlers in Nebraska build homes of sod?

17. According to the 1995 *Guinness Book of World Records*, where is the world's largest classification railroad yard located?

18. During World War II, how many soldiers were greeted and fed by volunteers when their troop trains stopped at the North Platte Canteen? a. six hundred, b. six thousand, c. six million

19. Can you name Nebraska's state bird, state flower, and state tree?

20. Nebraska, the name of the state, is derived from a Native American word for the Platte River meaning "flat or broad water." True or False?

Answers

1. Arbor Day

2. Rodeo

3. Nebraska is known as the "Cornhusker State" because of the importance of corn.

4. Sandhill crane

5. Missouri

6. Febold Feboldson

7. 160 acres

8. False...the mammoth is the state fossil.

9. President Abraham Lincoln, our 16th

10. "Unicameral" means one house. The Nebraska legislature has only one house, the senate. The other 49 state legislatures are divided into two houses: the house of representatives and the senate.

11. Kool-Aid®

12. A powwow is a social celebration of Native American rituals and traditions that includes dancing, singing, drumming and colorful regalia.

13. Approximately 76,000 people

14. Father Flanagan

15. Chimney Rock, Scotts Bluff, Jail Rock, Courthouse Rock

16. Since trees were scarce on the plains, the settlers were forced to use the prairie itself, or thick ribbons of grass and soil, for their building material.

17. North Platte, Nebraska

18. c. six million

19. Western meadowlark bird, goldenrod flower, and cottonwood tree

20. True

Rajean Luebs Shepherd

Rajean Luebs Shepherd spent happy childhood days growing up in Bay City, Michigan near Lake Huron. Upon graduating from Central Michigan University with a degree in elementary education, the world became her classroom as she traveled for 10 years and performed with the international, educational, musical organization, Up with People.

Rajean resides in North Platte, Nebraska with her husband, Stuart, and her two sons, Breton and Collin. She loves her job as a substitute teacher and enjoys sharing her favorite children's books with her students. Rajean is excited to showcase the great state of Nebraska with her first children's book, *C is for Cornhusker: A Nebraska Alphabet.*

Sandy Appleoff

Illustration veteran Sandy Appleoff calls home a third generation farm in Falls City, Nebraska. Currently she is teaching and working on an MFA in stage and costume design at the University of Kansas. Over 20 years in commercial illustration her work has appeared in a range of venues from corporate advertising, to magazines, to children's books, to large-scale installation murals. Sandy's teaching career has also included the Kansas City Art Institute and Colorado Mountain College in Aspen.

Sandy's cover art is loosely based on Appleoff Acres.